Peace

by

Piece

A step-by-step guide to putting your life back together when grief tears it apart

by

Dr. Roneisa Matero

Copyright

is not intended to diagnose, treat or cure any disease or illness. For
diagnosis or treatment of any medical problem, consult your own
physician.

Table of Contents

Letter to Reader

Dear Reader,

I want to take a moment to thank you for picking up this book and for being willing and having the courage to change the way you think about grief and the grieving process. Thank you for choosing to walk the path to healing your broken heart and start putting your life back together even when all you want to do is curl up in a ball and shut yourself off from the world. Because after a sudden and unexpected loss of a loved one, your world is forever changed and definitely not the way you had planned. I remember when my husband passed away suddenly in a plane crash, I felt like my whole life was over. And in a lot of ways it was. He was only 31 years old and in the Special Forces division of the USAF. I was 30 years old and our children were 5 and 7 at the time. I was devastated and I was mad at God for taking him from us.

As I look back and reflect on how much I cried which at first seemed like all day every day and got mad and wanted to give up, all I had to do was look at my children and I knew I had to go on and somehow stay strong for them. Speaking of crying all the time, I guess it had been about six months since Chris died and I was upstairs in my closet looking at some cards and letters he had sent me and the kids while he was deployed to Afghanistan. I was crying as I was reading the cards and letters, and as I looked up from one of the letters, I saw both Brianna and Dante standing there looking at me, they both began to cry, and said, *"mommy please don't cry anymore."* It was in that moment I decided I had to be strong for them and that I needed to cry less in their presence. I soon found myself crying every morning in the shower so my children would not see me cry. This became my time to pray and release my pain as the tears were washed away with the water in the shower. For a little while in the mornings I would feel better, but it didn't take long for my mind to start replaying that early morning on August 7, 2002 when I got the news that would forever change not only my life, but my children's lives forever.

I was standing in my doorway looking out my front door at 5 military personnel from the Air Force base at my door and they looked at me and said, "I'm sorry Mrs. Matero" and put their heads down. Now, any military wife knows what it means when you are visited by several personnel in their dress uniforms. I put my head down and said, "I know you are not here to tell me what I think you are here to tell me?" Then my world shattered.

I tell you this to let you know that I am a real person who has real thoughts, feelings and emotions such as fear, pain, heartache, suicidal thoughts, anger, guilt, and shame, just to name a few. I have lived and I am still living the everyday struggle to keep my mind from dragging me back down into the deep dark hole of my looping negative thought patterns that seem to be relentless when in the depths of the grieving process. You see I didn't just relive that morning I got the news, I could not stop thinking about how unfair it was and how bad I hurt. I hurt for my children too. My pain felt unbearable at times, my chest hurt so bad, and my heart felt like it had been shattered in a million pieces. I would think about what was missing, and the important life events that our children were going to have that he was supposed to be a part of.

The more I thought about all the ways my life was over, the more negative thoughts would evolve and give me more reason to stay mad and sad and cry out to God and ask, "Why me and why do my children have to grow up without their father?" "How am I supposed to raise them on my own?" I prayed (ok maybe yelled at God) every day to help me and guide me to do what was needed to raise my children and for the guidance and strength to keep going and be the best mom I could for them.

This went on for many years, by the way, I thought I was supposed to cry and mourn the loss of my husband forever. Yes, I would do my best to stay strong for my children the best I could because I didn't want them to think I couldn't handle everything and raise them on my own. I wanted them to see me as supportive, loving, strong, courageous, and know that I loved them more than anything in the world and that I made raising them and giving them the best possible life, my life's mission. There was one very important thing that I overlooked while raising my children and I didn't realize this until after they were grown. You see I was so busy raising them and trying to provide the best possible life for them, that I never stopped to realize I was living in survival mode and my mind was on auto pilot to think whatever it wanted. Our mindset is made up of what our mind is thinking, usually without us even knowing, I got caught up in the negative thought patterns of my grief and the painful event of losing my husband that changed our lives forever.

What I mean to say is, I didn't realize my mind was replaying the negative, unhealthy thoughts like a record over and over because they had become so familiar that it just felt normal for me to be sad, and after all, I was still grieving. Now, don't get me wrong I had some fun and happy times with my children, and they have grown up to be the most loving, caring, respectful, giving humans I could have ever imagined. But there was always this looming reality that something (their dad) was missing. I can't tell you how many times they would say "mom I sure wish daddy was here." And all I could say is "me too honey, me too." Usually with tears running down my face, actually that is happening right now as I write you this letter.

Speaking of that, crying is our body's way of releasing what we need to release, and the pain, hurt, and heartache, we feel when we are grieving has to be released before we can begin to heal. I believe that once we start to really feel and then release those feelings and emotions, it is then that our mind and our heart can connect. And that my friend is where we can start to heal in a way, we never thought possible. It is then that we become aware of the fact that what we think determines how we feel, and when we can begin to reach for more positive thoughts, we begin to feel better. Oh, my goodness, this took me so long to understand this.

My mind and unknowingly my mindset was keeping me in the negative, depressed, crappy mood, because it had become so conditioned to think the same negative thoughts over and over again, which in turn affected how I felt inside and because how we feel on the inside is reflected in how we show up in the world on the outside, I didn't like what I saw when I looked in the mirror. I look back now and I am glad I realized that it didn't have to be that way and I could change what I was thinking and feeling instead of continuing to live my life in sadness and pain.

Why am I telling you all this? Well, I don't want you to spend years living in the negative thought patterns that keep you stuck in your grief, feeling depressed and like life is not worth living like I did. What I am going to share with you on the pages of this book will help you understand how our mind and our mindset determines how we feel and how what we feel determines what we do in life. Can you see how this all works together and if left to chance it can lead us to a life of pain and sorrow? Now, I am not telling you that you should not grieve the loss of your spouse or important loved one. But what I am telling you is once you decide to feel those emotions of grief, let them settle and then release them instead of holding on and reliving the pain and letting your negative thought pattern surrounding the loss determine how you feel, you will begin to experience more joy and eventually happiness again.

That is my wish for you along your healing journey, and I am so glad you decided to pick up this book and that you will use the PEACE method, tips and tools to assist you along your life's ever-changing path. Just remember, it doesn't happen overnight, but with a little dedication and consistency using these tips from my healing journey, you too will begin to heal and learn to live again.

I am sending you love and blessings,
Roneisa

"You can shed tears because they are gone, or you can
smile because they lived.
You can close your eyes and pray they will come
back, or you can open your eyes and see all that they
left for you.
Your heart can be empty because you can't see them,
or you can be full of the love you shared.
You can turn your back on tomorrow and relive
yesterday, or you can be happy for tomorrow because of
yesterday.
You can remember only that they are gone, or you can
cherish their memory and let it live on.
You can cry and close your mind and feel empty, or
you can do what they would want. Smile, Open your
heart. Love.... and go on."

~Elizabeth Ammons

Chapter 1 - Introduction

Our Mindset in Grief

Once your mindset changes, everything on the outside

will change along with it.

~Steve Maraboli

What is our mindset anyway? How do you describe the mind and your mindset? A set of assumptions, notations, or simply, the way a person thinks. The American Heritage dictionary defines our mindset as "a fixed mental attitude or disposition that predetermines a person's responses to and interpretations of situations; an inclination or a habit; a way of thinking; an attitude or opinion, especially a habitual one." When we think about this definition of our mind and mindset then we could reasonably assume that our mindset or the thoughts we think, is made up of our past beliefs and situations.

A strong mindset has the power to attract things that are in harmony with it. Our mindset shapes all our views and is made up of our beliefs and a belief is just a thought that we keep thinking over and over again. Our beliefs are made up of our past experiences. Our mind is programmed to think thoughts that are familiar and the thoughts surrounding the events, whether good or bad, that have happened in our life are what is familiar.

If our mindset is a way of thinking; an attitude or disposition that predetermines a person's responses to situations in our lives, then where did we get the attitude and way of thinking? Studies in psychology have shown that our mindset on certain things is already developed early on by our parents and caregivers, some areas develop later as we come across new situations. When we go through the pain of a sudden loss, whether in childhood or later in our life, such as the loss of a loved one, we develop a mindset around grief and that determines how we will respond to situations that cause us to grieve in the future. Addressing the pain of loss is difficult.

Pain is not a single emotion,

rather we feel like we are standing in the rain

and every raindrop that washes over us

comes with a different emotion.

Anger, sadness, guilt, loss, you name it, and you find it in that storm of anguish. We are drenched from head to toe, and there is no ray of hope which can clear the mess and take us out of our vulnerability.

When the unexpected happens such as when we lose one of our parents, spouse, a sibling, or even the tragic loss of one of our children, our mind tries to protect us by going into what I call "survival mode". It's like our bodies and mind shift into auto pilot. When we are in survival mode our minds get overwhelmed and we try to keep ourselves busy by such things as working all the time, shutting down and sleeping all day, overeating, or turning to drugs or alcohol so we don't have to think (listen to the chatter of our mindset) about our lives now without our loved one, the future we have lost with them, or how we will go on in life.

The loss and grief that comes when you lose your spouse or your beloved (what happened to me) can feel like your heart has been ripped out of your chest, and it doesn't matter if you had been together a few months or for many, many years. When we say, *'I do,'* we aren't just making a vow to accept the person for who he or she is, but also forging a bond of love, tolerance, and togetherness *till death do us part.* But what happens when the death of our spouse rips the charm out of our life? What happens when we no longer wake up to their smiling face every morning? When there is no one to call us for little things, or to share all sorts of secrets? We feel lost. We feel like there's nothing worth living for. This pain feels so much bigger and more intense. Because the loss is bigger than anything we've ever experienced before, this pain will naturally steer our mindset towards overwhelming negativity. Let me assure you…this is completely normal.

When we get married, or enter into any important loving relationship, our mindset of a lifelong relationship filled with love and tenderness is established. Even though we know that death is a harsh reality of life, we barely consider it when we are at the peak of happiness and busy building a life together. When we are drunk in love, we have the mindset that nothing can go wrong. As we tackle minor inconveniences, we think that nothing can break our bond, and nothing can pull us apart. And at that moment, when we're so high and strong in love, our worst fears of losing our loved ones never comes to life. Although, in my case, being the wife of a man who was in the Special Forces division of the military, my mind knew of the possibility that I could lose him on any given mission. But I would quickly dismiss those thoughts because I didn't want to live in fear.

Loss is traumatic and can make us go through a lot of pain and anguish. The loss of love and tenderness is something we will be aware of our whole life. When you are a young widow with kids, you are constantly toiling between healing yourself and taking care of your kids. In the process you have to be aware of your feelings and pain as well as stay strong for your children. This takes immense courage. And with courage, it takes a sane mindset to set things straight in your life. If we decide to keep reminiscing on old memories of our loved ones, it will make us yearn to relive those moments instead of healing ourselves and living right now.

Usually, our mindset is made up of our past beliefs and situations. A healthy, strong mindset has the power to attract things that are in harmony with it. It is like a flexible mirror. A lot of times, grief makes the mirror foggy. The loss makes everything seem blurry.

When the unthinkable happens,
the pain of loss is overwhelming,
but it's the mindset surrounding the loss
that adds to your suffering.

The negative mindset bound with grief will only make it worse. A positive mindset will help you to turn the grief into an opportunity for self-reflection and growth. The purpose of this book is to help your mind grow with positive affirmations and tools to help you leave the negative mindset behind.

A smell, a song, or a laugh, anything could bring

that instant feeling of sorrow, pain, and grief. Feeling that way is fine, being vulnerable is fine, crying, sobbing, screaming, and running…all fine and even normal in the grieving process. That is being real, but don't let the fear break you. Life can be understood backward, but it can only be lived forward.

The peace will come from the memories
that make your heart sink today.

If you carry on with denial and isolation, then you will miss the cure of grief and will be trapped within its confines forever. The truth is that our loss gets integrated into our daily lives and routines over time. Our mind will always carve a new life out of it and each person's experience is different. The new life will be different from the previous one, but hopefully, with a positive mindset and a bit of time it can become a positive transformation.

Remember, it's okay to cry or sob or run away from people while you are in distress. Understand that your grieving process is unique. Don't be too harsh on yourself. It's a long road when it comes to dealing with the loss of someone you deeply loved. There is no shortcut. You have to go through each step, turn by turn, to arrive at your destination. Allow yourself some time to go through the steps moving at your pace. Give yourself space to understand that you may feel as if you are not in control of your emotions. Never deny the fact that you are grieving.

Suppressed emotions only lead to self-destruction.

You might become anxious, depressed, and enraged. You could also develop harmful habits like overeating, drugs, violence, and sometimes even suicidal thoughts. I worked hard through the grieving process. But what I found was that by changing my mindset around my grief, I was able to heal my heart and move forward one piece at a time. By implementing the transformative 5 simple steps of the P.E.A.C.E. method outlined in the coming chapters, you will be able to take control of your mind and thoughts as you pause, recognize, examine, acknowledge, change, and expand your mindset to live a more positive fulfilling life.

To those who are grieving, you are not alone. We stand together. I know that it feels like a part inside you is dead. But as life goes on… know that I am by your side. The sun still rises; the wind still blows. The world keeps on spinning at its own speed. But how can you move on after something has happened that you didn't even want to think about? When it feels like everything that you have now is empty arms and a mind filled with echoing memories, leaving you alone for a moment and returning the very next one. My prayer is that you will use the tips and tools in the next chapters of this book to be more aware of your negative thoughts and feelings surrounding your grief and move though the grieving process with a knowing that you are not alone, and that you can do it. You are stronger than you think you are and more capable than you know. Don't believe me, give it a try, you may just surprise yourself. You got this! I am here for you and walking with you every step of the way.

Chapter 2 -
My Expertise

I learned that, with grief, you have to take it one day at a time and learn how to find the happiness amid the heartbreak.

~Adrienne C. Moore

Turning to the other side of the bed through the sleepless night, the reality again hits you hard. Life becomes merciless sometimes. Living with something that you feared the most is not that easy. The reality is even worse. You are in pain, and it can't get better. Life didn't unfold the way you wanted it to, and your happiness has vaporized.

07 August 2002 – my whole world collapsed around me when I got the news that a plane crashed in the mountains of Puerto Rico, and my husband Technical Sergeant, Christopher Matero, a combat controller in the USAF, departed from this world, leaving me and our two beautiful children, who were ages 5 and 7, behind. The thought of living without him was terrifying, and now

here I was, living it. My worst fear had come to fruition just when I thought everything was coming together. I lost him when we were in the best part of our lives. I had recently completed my education with my master's degree as a Family Nurse Practitioner, and our life was finally starting to settle down. Chris had gotten off of active-duty status in the USAF, so he could spend more time at home, and we could raise our children together. We had just bought our dream home in Greenville, Indiana that we planned on raising our children in just three months before his death.

Words could never explain how I really felt at that time. Isolated, angry, sad, alone, scared out of my mind, and confused. However, *I asked myself several times, was grief the only thing I had from him?* The answer was no. Sorrow wasn't the only thing he left behind for me. He passed his legacy to me, and to our children. He left behind a bouquet of memories that made me feel alive and loved every time I relived them and still do, to this day. The mountain trips, the long walks on the beach, and spending the week after my graduation at Kuai Hawaii… every memory was, and still is, a treasure. Most people cry remembering those memories, but they forget that the best thing about memories is making them. I am happy with the fact that at least memories last forever.

Being alive with such a feeling of sorrow is hard for our hearts and our minds to carry after the loss of our loved one. Our heart gets broken in many ways that can't be fixed. The one thing that always kept me moving was the fact that I got a chance to live life with him, even if it was only a short time. I tried looking for a silver lining – and failed – until I realized what a blessing it was to have lived with him for the years he was alive, leaving me with memories that I could live with and cherish forever and share with our children and grandchildren.

Grief is a new territory for everyone, as there is no specific way to behave according to it and no real timeline. The process is entirely personal. We live in a culture that actually doesn't talk about the real scope of grief. We know that the reality of grief is different from what others see or guess from the outside. Sometimes there is no reason for things that have already occurred as we look back along our own grief journey. The silver lining is not always visible to you. Explanations don't work here. But we have to start somewhere to learn about loss, love, and grief in order to understand and start to heal and grow through it.

Pain and love travel hand in hand,
and they will always co-exist.

However, little by little, the pain will get easier to carry, I promise. After all, it doesn't feel good or bad to have survived and been left with this mess that sudden and unexpected loss leaves behind. I am sorry that you have to learn it the hard way. But as you go through the grieving process you will find out soon that our mindset and the negative thoughts and feelings surrounding grief can be allowed to come and we can acknowledge them, sit with them, and then heal from them with a more positive mindset and thought pattern. It will be a life of your own making, the most beautiful way it could be possible. You only need to find the thread of love that is still there in your heart. Just think if your spouse or loved one was alive, would they be happy to see you like this? You know the answer already.

At the time of this writing, Chris has been gone for over 18 years. Since then, life has not been easy for me nor our children to cope and survive through the years. I have raised my children, and they are now healthy, loving, compassionate grown adults and both are happily married with amazing spouses. Brianna has two beautiful children named Peyton, who is 4 and Weston, who is 2 years old. They are such a blessing to our family. They give me so much joy and happiness that I did not have for many years and honestly, didn't expect to ever have again when I was deep in the throes of my grief. I was stuck in my grief and was not allowing myself to heal. I was so focused on raising my children that I did not think about or realize that I was ignoring my feelings and emotions just to survive and push through my pain. I now realize that we have to take the time to feel our emotions in order to heal from them. We have to move through the grieving process one step at a time to come out on the other side stronger and with a healed heart and with a new-found understanding to forever cherish the love we shared with our loved one.

Sometimes, I still wrestle with grief, and there

were times I wanted to die badly. But love is a powerful emotion. Use the power inside it so that you can start breathing slowly and deeply again and begin to heal your broken heart, one piece at a time. Grief cannot be shared. Everyone carries their own burden alone on their way. Learn to take one moment at a time like I did, by becoming aware of what I was thinking and feeling and slowly changing my negative thoughts and feelings to positive ones. Use the power inside you to begin breathing slowly and deeply again and begin to heal your broken heart, one piece at a time.

Join me in this journey beyond grief – let's work our way through the sorrow, pain, and bereavement together. In this book, I will teach you how to breathe again and mend your broken heart using the 5 step P.E.A.C.E method I developed while healing along my own grief journey. It is my sincere hope that this book can help you move forward along your ever-changing grief journey by developing a better understanding of the human mind and our mindset around grief. Our mindset that is made up of our predetermined thoughts and feelings surrounding how we respond to and react to grief and how we navigate through the grieving process. If you implement these principles and tools in this book you can overcome your negative thought patterns around grief by changing your mindset. And, let me tell you, once you become more aware of your thoughts and apply these simple steps on how to change them, your life will change.

Chapter 3 -
The P.E.A.C.E. Framework

The only way to make sense out of change is to plunge into it, move with it, and join the dance.

~Alan Watts

It's all about mindset. All I want is for you to understand the role our mind and our mindset play in our daily battle with grief and for you to be able to change, grow and evolve through the process. I am not happy that you are here, but I am glad that you will be reading further and that you are ready to face your pain and grief, change your mind, and heal your heart to change your life.

After a severe loss, it is hard to venture any new hope. We are so consumed by our loss. We feel like the world is oblivious to our sufferings. Stunned, confused, and angry… we blink in utter disbelief. The past still triggers us. For those of us who have lost a spouse, you still miss how they used to bring you flowers on birthdays, and how you enjoyed dancing in the living room to your favorite songs. If you are a parent who has lost a child, you miss hearing them call for you in the middle of the night or kissing you on the cheek and telling you how much they love you. Or, if you have suffered the loss of a parent or sibling, you long for their guidance, love and comfort. To be able to just pick up the phone and call them one more time for advice or just talk about anything to hear their voice.

While you wonder how you can bear all those years ahead without them, know that our human mind is working at a subconscious level to keep us safe and on the best possible outcome. I know from experience that there are moments when we are grieving the loss of our loved one that we wonder if we are ever going to heal our broken heart. When we are stuck in the past and reliving the pain of our loss over and over in our minds with our negative thought patterns, our mind cannot work towards the goal that is to heal.

There are a lot of times in our life when we become vulnerable, and everything reminds us about our grief, making wounds bleed again, reminding us of what we have lost, triggering our mind to spiral down into the depths of our negative thoughts and feelings again. I found through my own grief journey that it is cyclic, and it comes and goes like the waves of the ocean one after the other. At times we feel like we cannot bear it, and this will never end. We can't let them go. The shock, denial, anger, guilt, the numbness – and then you find that there is no place to go to escape the pain of grief. This is the time when you start isolating yourself. You just want to run and hide from everything. You think that there is no place to go to escape the pain and sadness of your grief.

No matter what situation you are experiencing right now, what words you have just exchanged, what loss you have just gone through. Take a deep breath and stay focused on what you know right now. There is always a lesson for you to learn, you will always have something to gain from your experiences in life. No lesson is easy to learn, whether that be from our own experiences, or from others. However, you need to trust yourself, it might look and feel hard at the time, but have faith and you will always find it. When you find it, you learn to grow from it. That is how you can make space for something good to come from something that made you suffer. This reminds me of one of my favorite quotes by

Louise Hay, it says *"Everything is working out for my highest good. Out of this situation only good will come. I am safe."*

For many years I grieved and felt stuck in my grief, like I just couldn't move forward for fear that I would forget Chris. I don't know if you have that same fear of forgetting your loved one, but for me it was so powerful that I just couldn't stop thinking about him, and that he was no longer here to live life with me and our children. I thought if I stopped hurting that I would stop feeling the love I had with him. I know that might sound crazy, but I really thought that to keep his memory alive in my heart it had to be painful. I now know that I can still love him and hold him in my heart with a sense of peace and joy, remembering the love we shared and good memories we made together and as a family.

One early morning, I can't remember the exact day, as I was sitting quietly and praying to God to help me find a way to heal from my pain, help me feel better, and to be a better mother, I had an overwhelming urge to sit down and write in my journal. I started writing whatever came to my mind and as I did the words and processes of what I now call the P.E.A.C.E. method to healing pain and grief were scribbled on the pages. Although, I did not know at the time what these words would mean or how I would use them to change my life, I began slowly implementing those simple steps I had written down in my journal that day. After all what did I have to lose, I already felt defeated and depressed, and all I wanted was to feel better so I could be a happier person for myself and my children.

Through my painful journey and struggles with grief God showed me a way, a simple process to change my thoughts, to help me stop living in that downward spiral of grief and negative thoughts. Those words in my journal became known as the 5-step process that I call the P.E.A.C.E. method for changing our negative thoughts to positive ones. This process changed my mindset and my life and I want to share it with you in the hope that it will save you from the years of pain and suffering I went through before I discovered that I didn't have to live in pain and be depressed for the rest of my life. I only wish I had asked God for help sooner. If you are asking for help right now, I pray this is the answer to your prayers. This mindfulness method takes some time and dedication, as nothing worth changing happens overnight. But if practiced, it will change your perception, your mindset, and ultimately your life. Change your perception – change your life!

The P.E.A.C.E Method is a five-step mental checklist that you can use anytime you want to get out of a negative thinking spiral and replace it with positive energy and creative thoughts. So, why do we need to change our thoughts and our mindset, and why do we need to practice it? Well first of all we must understand how our mind works and that our mindset affects every aspect of our lives from our moods to ultimately our personality. What I found through my research and my own experience, is that when we are grieving our mind tends to focus on the pain and loss of what once was and what we lost and can never get back. As I shared earlier in this chapter, I was stuck for many years in the negative thought patterns of my grief because I didn't know there was a way to change my thoughts. Like me and for most of us that leads to negative feelings such as sadness, anger, guilt, and shame to name a few. These negative feelings and thought patterns can lead us to depression and isolation. I do not want that for you. So let me introduce you to the P.E.A.C.E. method and a way to start healing your mind to heal your broken heart.

The P.E.A.C.E. METHOD

P- Pause and Ponder and become aware of your current thoughts and beliefs around grief

E- Examine and explore your current thought or feeling to see where you feel it in your body

A- Acknowledge and accept the feelings and thoughts that are there- you are feeling them even if you consciously do not want to think or feel that way

C- Change and correct/redirect the feeling or thought to a positive feeling or thought

E- Elevate and expand the positive thought or feeling to keep it present in your mind (repetition is key)

Let's start with the "P" in the P.E.A.C.E. method. The "P" stands for "Pause and Ponder". To stop and pause to ponder over a thought or feeling we are having, and to become aware of what our mind is thinking at that given moment. Awareness is the first step in healing.

The "E" in the P.E.A.C.E. method represents our ability to "Examine or Explore" the feeling that we have identified and become aware of during our pause moment. When we examine a feeling or a thought, we should go within ourselves and feel the experience.

The "A" in the P.E.A.C.E. method stands for "Acknowledge or Accept" that the feeling or thought is there, and it is there for a reason. Our mind does what is familiar and if negative, fearful thoughts are in our mind frequently, our mind will automatically reach for the familiar thoughts even if they are negative. In order to change our negative thoughts, we have to feel them and acknowledge them so that we develop our awareness surrounding them.

The "C" in the P.E.A.C.E method represents our need to "Change or Correct" our negative thoughts and feelings and replace them with positive, uplifting thoughts and feelings. This for me was the hardest part of my healing journey. Our mind does not want us to change, because it is trying to keep us safe or at least our subconscious mind thinks it is. In our mind familiar is safe, and unfamiliar things such as positive thoughts and feelings are unsafe. Especially when we are in the depths of our grief.

The final "E" in the P.E.A.C.E. method stands for "Elevate or Expand" our positive thoughts and feelings to more positive thoughts and feelings in order to change our mood, and ultimately our mindset. If we can expand and think more positive thoughts which in turn produce positive feelings, our body will respond to help us heal. This is when the mind and heart are working together and that is when the magic happens.

Chapter 4 -
P - Pause and Ponder

Give yourself the permission to pause to create sacred space

— the space to consciously choose how you want to respond

to any situation.

~Dr. Debra Reble

When I talk about the "P" in the P.E.A.C.E. method, I want to explain that what I mean by pause and ponder is to become mindful of your thoughts and feelings and just be in the present. Being mindful means to slow down and become aware of how you feel and the thoughts that you are thinking, especially when you are in the middle of your grief and the same thoughts and feelings, that usually cause pain and sorrow, keep coming back over and over again. When our mind is overwhelmed by grief and the loss of our loved one, it can get stuck in the loop of negativity and negative thinking without us even being aware that it is happening and suddenly, we are feeling really bad emotionally and physically as well. This happens because our mind keeps going back to what is familiar and following a loss so great as losing a spouse, or important loved one, the pain is so overwhelming and intense that it is felt in our whole body. Our mind is trying to find a solution to ease our pain but can only rehearse the thoughts we have been thinking – our past experiences and then translate that into body sensations and negative emotions, thoughts and feelings. When we are hurting from our loss and in pain, those emotions such as shame, guilt, anger, and sadness can be so intense and never ending, that we don't know how to make them stop or ease the pain.

To pause means to physically take a "time out" from whatever you are doing and get still and quiet and be present in your own body and in that particular moment in time. Some may refer to the act of sitting quietly as meditation or prayer. Meditation is best known as a habitual process of getting still and training your mind to focus and redirect your thoughts. This is a perfect way to begin our first step in the P.E.A.C.E. method process to pause and ponder. Before I begin, I usually find a comfortable place to sit or lie down, I close my eyes and take three slow deep breaths to help me focus and calm my mind so I can listen and recognize the thoughts in my mind and feel the feelings that I am having at that moment. When I am sitting quietly, or meditating, I am observing what is going on with my body to see if I feel any discomfort or tightness somewhere in my body. Usually, when I can feel a tightness or uneasiness in my body it is a direct response to what I am thinking in my mind. Especially if I am unconsciously rehearsing the negative and painful events of my past over and over. My body starts to feel anxious, and sometimes I even have chest pain. It is amazing how much our physical body reacts to what is going on in our mind.

Daily practice will give you a lot of benefits such as reducing mental and physical stress, improve your mood, improved sleep when done before bed, lower your blood pressure and improve your overall health. If you are new to the art of taking a "time out" or sitting quietly with your thoughts and feelings and wondering how the heck do I meditate? Here are the steps to help you begin your meditation practice. Practice it daily to see a change.

EASY STEPS FOR TAKING A "TIME OUT" TO PAUSE AND PONDER OR MEDITATE:

- Sit on a chair or on the floor, with your back straight and in a stable position. Or you can lie down on your back if that is more comfortable for you.

- Keep your legs steady in front of you if sitting in a chair or crossed if sitting on the floor. If you are lying down, just relax with legs straight or you can slightly raise them and bend your knees if that is more comfortable for you. Keep your spine as straight as possible.

- Just relax, don't stiffen your body but keep your back as straight as possible.

- Let your upper arms stay parallel to your body. Relax your arms by your side. You can touch your index finger and thumb together if you would like to. You can also relax your hands on your thighs if sitting and let your hands rest open and palms facing upward.

- With your back as straight as possible, slightly lower your chin and let your eyes fall downwards slowly and gently.

- Just stay like this and relax for a few moments, feel your body as it sinks into the chair, bed, or floor. Do this for about 15 minutes, but you can relax and get calm for as long as your body needs to, or time allows.

- Repeat it - Whenever you feel like you need a break from the world.

According to Dr. Joe Dispenza, best-selling author and chiropractor, most of our thoughts and feelings come from our past experiences and our brain is a record of everything we have experienced throughout our lives. Whenever we have an experience in our life, we use our five senses to determine how we will react to that same experience the next time it happens because we have formed an imprint in the brain for that experience. He suggests that our thoughts are the language of the brain and feelings are the language of the body. He goes on to say that how we think and how we feel creates a state of being, and in order to change our state of being, we have to change how we think and how we feel.

We often get stuck in our own heads and in our thoughts, preventing ourselves from moving forward with life, and this can be especially true when we are grieving and trying to make sense of our new reality. And for most of us, it is a reality we never wanted or thought we would be experiencing. This new reality that determines how we think and how we feel, can eventually become our new state of being. If we can take the time to stop and pause for a few minutes and get to a higher level of awareness within our minds by using meditation as a tool, we can recognize what we are feeling and the thoughts that are going on in our head. By recognizing and being aware that we are thinking these negative thoughts and feeling a certain way we can pause more often and think about something positive in our life and begin to change our current state of being.

It can be hard to stay in the present moment, because it may be painful, but it's good to start as early as possible along your grief journey, so you are not dwelling and constantly thinking about your past. You are just living one mindful moment at a time. When you begin practicing mindfulness and living in the present moment, you will feel more positivity entering your life. This practice also helps in reducing negative self-talk. What you really need to learn about mindfulness is that it is not obscure, you don't need to change for it. Meditating for mindfulness involves taking time to pay attention to where we are and what is actually happening around us. That starts with being aware of our presence and body. This act is very soothing as our body has rhythms that help it to relax.

The pain of loss is overwhelming, but it's our mindset that develops from our grief that adds to our suffering. The negative mindset bound with our grief will only make it worse. A positive mindset, and being present in each moment, not living in the past, will help you to turn the grief into an opportunity for self-reflection and growth. And as a result, we can grow out of the pain into a new person with a new outlook on life. One that makes life worth living again.

Pause/Ponder Practice:

Sometimes the simple act of recognizing and naming a body sensation and the emotion associated with it can be a very liberating and soothing practice when we are first grieving. We call this, 'name it and claim it' and it can be done while walking, meditating, or even doing the dishes or the laundry. It is a simple mindfulness exercise of scanning your body and noticing what sensations you feel and where and then noticing any emotions that you also feel. In this way you begin to add a mindful awareness and self-care to your body and emotional state by the simple and gentle act of paying attention.

For example:
Name it (body sensation): I feel tightness and tension in my shoulders
Claim it (emotion): I feel sad and burdened

Name it (body sensation):

Claim it (emotion):

Name it (body sensation):

Claim it (emotion):

Pause:

Pause now for a few moments
and reflect on the quote below.

---

*The soul always knows what to do to
heal itself. The challenge is to silence
the mind. ~Caroline Myss*

As you pause, what feels like one thing you could do to
begin your own healing process?

What are some of the most natural ways that you already
know quiet and calm your mind?

Ponder:

Ponder and reflect on the quote below

for a few moments.

Grief never ends, but it changes. It's
not a place to stay. Grief is not a sign
of weakness, nor a lack of faith. It is
the price of love. ~Unknown

How does the quote speak to your own grief journey so far?

Have you ever judged yourself because you are grieving?

In those moments of self-judgement, what kinder and more loving thoughts could you say to yourself?

Chapter 5 - E- Examine and Explore

Sometimes you have to experience what you don't want to in life to come to a full understanding of what you do want.

~Mandy Hale

The next step in the P.E.A.C.E. method is the "E". It represents the time we take to examine and explore our thoughts and feelings that we recognized while we prayed and meditated and took the time to pause our minds in the previous step. What does it mean to examine and explore our thoughts and feelings? For me it means to sit with these feelings and thoughts, and this can be done during the prayer and meditation time you learned about in the pause and ponder step of the process. When I am praying and meditating and following the P.E.A.C.E. method of calming my mind and working on changing my mindset, I usually block off about 30 to 60 minutes for myself. I have to put it in my calendar so I make time to do it.

My usual morning routine consists of my quiet time before anyone else wakes up. This is my time for me to get my mind right and is part of my self-care routine to start my day with the best possible mindset I can so I can be the best possible version of myself throughout the day. If I don't do it first thing in the morning, I have a difficult time finding the "time" to do it throughout my busy day. During this time for myself, I spend time in prayer and meditation so that I can start my day with God and a positive, grateful attitude and mindset to carry me throughout the day. This practice helps me to start my day without dragging the troubles and pain of yesterday with me into each new day. As I said, it is a practice. It is a conscious choice to clear our mind and do our best to start each new day with positive thoughts and a positive mindset. Being grateful for what we have is a great place to start.

As you learn to keep yourself centered and bring awareness to those unbearable feelings of grief, you can begin to make small changes in your mindset, which will eventually bring less pain and healing to your broken heart. By using the tips, tools and the P.E.A.C.E. process outlined throughout this book you will overcome the negative mindset of grief and despair and begin to see that grief does not have to be your everyday reality. When the waves of sadness and helplessness wash over you and you initially feel the emotion and its depth, start to breathe through the grief with slow deep breaths. This will help you stay grounded and bring you back to the present and out of the past.

Another tool that can help you examine and explore your feelings and thoughts is practicing mindfulness. *Ask yourself, mind full or mindful?* Your body is present here, is your mind here? Mindfulness is something that everyone possesses naturally, but most of us are either out of practice or have never been taught how to practice mindfulness. Whenever a person brings awareness to what they are experiencing at the moment or to their state of mind with thoughts and emotions, this is being mindful. While doing grounding practices such as meditation, yoga, or even walks in nature, remember to be present and feel your emotions and the feelings associated with your current experience. This is how you begin to practice mindfulness.

Mindfulness = Meditation + breathe + balance + stress reduction + awareness + body and soul

Mindfulness is not about being positive all the time or feeling happy. It is about focusing on what is happening in the moment, feeling your feelings and recognizing your thoughts so you can sit and experience them fully and then move on to start to change them to a more positive experience. Being mindful is about getting from one moment to the next, from the difficult and painful to the easy and the moments full of joy. *It's all about building a muscle to be present and being awake in your life.*

Grief is cyclical and can sometimes change with the seasons, even when we are in the depths of winter, we know that eventually, it will become more manageable with the advent of spring. Learn to tolerate and pace yourself through the most severe times. Be good to yourself and forgive yourself for those times you don't have it all together. While you are experiencing your feelings and sitting with your thoughts around your grief, remember that self-care is so important to your healing journey. Repeat after me, '*Self-care is the most essential part even when you are grieving.*' Understandably, taking care of yourself is the last thing you want to do as you aren't even able to find the purpose of your life after the loss of your loved one. But we must do it in order to cope with the pain and move forward with life. And to do that, we need to be strong enough to indulge in self-care. Being kind, patient and self-nurturing to yourself may just be the best long-term skill and medicine that I can share with you.

So, let's talk a little bit about self-care. I mentioned self-care earlier as a part of my morning routine. I believe that it starts by listening to your body and mind. This is incorporated during the "E" step of the P.E.A.C.E. method of examining and exploring our thoughts as well as what our body is feeling in association to our thoughts. Our bodies will tell us what to do to heal. After going through such shock and loss when we suddenly and unexpectedly lose a loved one, our bodies show emotional, mental, physical, and spiritual symptoms. Our bodies need to be fed during this time to better handle the trauma. By this I don't just mean food,

I mean loving thoughts and feelings toward ourself as well for mind, body and soul healing to take place. When we are feeling the painful emotions of grief such as shame, guilt, anger, and sadness it is easy to take those feelings into our body as our own and it can lead to self-destructive behaviors. That is why self-care is so important during our grieving process.

HERE ARE SOME THINGS YOU CAN DO TO ENGAGE IN SELF-CARE DAILY:

- Get enough sleep. Make it a part of your self-care routine. It has a huge effect on how you feel physically and emotionally. It also reduces stress.

- Another thing that is a must on the-to-do list - taking care of your gut. Plan your daily meals and eat healthily. Go for fresh juices, fruits, and vegetables. The types of food you eat crucially impact the bacteria living in your digestive tract.

- After food, it's all about exercise. We already know that exercise is good for your health, but it also boosts your mood and reduces stress, sometimes as much as meditation. Try yoga or taking walks in nature. If you have the endurance, then maybe you can join the gym as well. Create a routine that works for you and makes you feel better.

When you suffer a trauma this big it's time to get back to the basics. We get so overwhelmed with the everyday task of grieving that we forget to do the little things that will help us the most to heal. First take time to breathe. I know we practice breathing during our meditation, but whenever you can, just stop, and take moment to take a few deep breathes, and let each breathe out slowly and feel how your body relaxes. You will be amazed at how this one seemingly small thing will change your state of being in an instant. Our bodies need oxygen to live and to heal. Breathing nourishes our body with the oxygen to sustain life. Rest whenever you get a chance. Take some time to do things that make you happy like take a soaking bath or take a walk out in nature. Try to maintain a regular sleep schedule. Take out some time to treat yourself properly, whatever makes you feel good, do that.

Only you can pull yourself out of this trauma.
So, to the best of your ability,
love yourself through your grief
by practicing daily self-care activities.

Examine/Explore Practice:

When a deep trauma or loss happens in your life, some days the best you can do is just breathe. Breathing returns us to our most elemental root, it grounds us in the here and now and breathing is very soothing to the body. As you become conscious of your breathing, you may notice how shallow it has been or that you haven't been breathing fully in your grief.

I encourage you to take a deep, full breath right now, all the way down to your belly. Place your hand over your belly and feel the breath enter and fill it.

- Breathe in for 5 counts (Inhale)

- Hold it for 2 counts

- Release for 5 counts (Exhale)

And if today, all you did was hold yourself together, I'm proud of you. If all you did today was breathe in and out and silently battle with the negative voice inside your head, then you should be proud of you too. ~Unknown

---

Examine:

---

*Work on being in love with the person
in the mirror who has been through so
much but it still standing.*
~Anonymous

Examine your expectations of yourself as you grieve...what expectations are you consciously or unconsciously holding yourself to? Are they working for you?

How could adopting a back to basics mindset give you some relief as you grieve?

What basics can you manage right now?

Explore:

---

*It takes a strong heart to love but it
takes a stronger heart to continue to
love after it's hurt. ~ Anonymous*

What feelings came up for you when you read in the
book, 'we need to be strong enough to indulge in self-
care?'

What self-care practices could you give yourself
permission to indulge in as you work through your grief?

How do you feel about your grief journey so far? Allow
yourself to write what you genuinely feel now, no
judgements or blame as you gently explore your feelings.

Chapter 6 - A- Acknowledge and Accept

Our intention creates our reality.

~Wayne Dyer

Once we have mastered the ability to become aware of our thoughts and feelings and be in the present moment as discussed in the previous steps for pause/ponder and examine/explore it is now time to implement the next step, which is the "A" in the P.E.A.C.E. method for healing our mindset and our heart. In this step we begin to acknowledge and accept our thoughts and feelings for what they are. Becoming aware and acknowledging our feelings and thoughts for what they are is an important step in changing our mindset. We as humans so often dismiss or push down our feelings and downplay our thoughts. When in reality, we should be paying attention and become more aware of what we think and how we feel each day. By acknowledging and accepting our feelings and thoughts as our body's way of communicating with us, we can become more in tune with our body, mind, and spirit.

When I came to the realization of my husband's death, I was shattered. I had never even imagined a life without him, I guess that's why they call it happily ever after. I had never looked beyond *'ever after.'* Yet his death served as a shocking reminder that nothing lasts forever, no matter how hard you try to hold on. Now that I look back, I realize that even though I was shattered and I couldn't move on for more than a decade, I gained a lot of experience through my pain. I had never wanted that to happen and I wouldn't want to even closely pass by that stage ever again. However, it deepened my compassion for others suffering from a similar loss. It made me realize that my life is not as shallow as I think. Over time, it broadened my vision and made me grateful for a lot of the things that have happened in my life. One of the most important things I realized is that even though I lost him, Chris made me a better person and brightened my life during the time we were together and gave me two amazing children to carry on his legacy, that still fill my life with love and joy each day.

As we move through these steps, we are changing our mindset one small step at a time and we can develop a mindset of positive thoughts and feelings, which leads to healing. First, acknowledge that everything happening around you is happening for you, not to you. Let the grieving mindset go and know that even being in this situation has something important *for you* even if you cannot fathom what that is right now. Accept that what you are thinking and feeling and what is happening to you is the way it is. I know that you never wanted it to be this way, but it is really important in ways you can't understand yet.

I believe to acknowledge and accept where we are is one of the most important steps in our healing process and also for changing our negative mindset to a more positive mindset. Don't fight against what has already happened, because living in the past and staying angry and mad will only keep us stuck in our negative mindset and pain of our grief. Don't beat yourself up for not being further along on your grief journey as you or others think you should be. Remember, our acknowledgment and acceptance of our thoughts and feelings, is just a step in the process of healing. But I will tell you that it is not easy to accept that our mindset is keeping us in the pain and not letting us heal. This is why it is so important to take time every day to sit in prayer and meditate and give yourself time to heal. Forgive your past and have gratitude for the time you got to spend with your spouse or loved one, focus on the good times. Visualize your body in a healed state, your mindset more positive, and that you will soon be doing better. Monitor your self-talk. What we say to ourselves in our mind makes a huge difference in our mindset. Take some deep breaths and calm yourself down when grief and anxiety hit you.

One of the greatest virtues of a happy life is gratitude. Ok, I know that right now you may be saying to yourself, *"how can I even think of being grateful when my heart is broken in a million pieces"?* But I am here to tell you from experience that when you start being grateful and thankful for all the good things that are in your life, instead of focusing on what is gone, you will be actively taking steps towards cultivating a more a positive mindset and life. This will also shift your attention from the negative side of life to the more happy and positive side. True happiness lies in living in the present while letting go of the past, but we have to first accept and acknowledge those feelings and thoughts in order to change them. The fragments of your past will still remain somewhere in your heart, popping up at random times, but be thankful for those memories you have now.

Most folks are as happy as they
make up their minds to be.
~Abraham Lincoln

I came across the above quote by accident, but when I read it, and read it again, I realized there was a lot of truth in just a few words. Throughout my grief journey, I have experienced this to be true of myself. We can decide to stay in our pain and sadness of our grief, or we can choose to accept our path and our past, learn from it and move forward with a grateful heart full of memories to share. It is just a choice. As you are able to choose to acknowledge and even accept your feelings and practice gratitude in your daily life, you will realize that there is a lot in your life to live for. Although nothing can fill the void of the loss of your beloved, you can begin to see beyond your loss and look for more positive aspects of your life. When you spend your days with an attitude of gratitude, you look at the brighter picture of your life.

If I may suggest one thing that has helped me to acknowledge and accept my thoughts and feelings, even when I didn't want to, and that is to journal or write down what I am feeling and thinking. And when I am finished, I then write a list of 5-10 things I am grateful for that day. This list can be anything you are grateful for in your life. I know when I started journaling, I would write the same things over and over every day and that is ok. Eventually, I was able to add more things to my list that I was grateful for each day as the weeks went on. Some people like to do this practice in the evening after their day is complete so they can reflect and thank God for what they are grateful for in their life. It doesn't matter if you do it in the morning, or evening, or even once a week, the important thing is that you do it. What I noticed as I have been journaling is that the more reasons I find to be grateful in my life, the more things show up to be grateful for each day. And my days got a little brighter.

I have heard throughout my life that *'writing is therapeutic'*, but I never realized just how much a simple task of writing down thoughts and feelings could help with the healing process and aid in our overall wellbeing. This practice becomes very important, especially when we are feeling alone and isolated. I recently read an article by Dr. Shelly Sommerfedt, a clinical psychologist, and she writes that journaling is a method of expressing and releasing thoughts and feelings. It can be a powerful tool for healing and can allow you to emotionally process what you have been dealing with. This essentially relieves the brain of holding all of these experiences within your mind and body and allows for release, which can be essential to healing and feeling better. Journaling allows you to be open and honest with yourself.

Please believe me when I say, *I understand that losing your loved one feels like you are stuck in a dark tunnel, with no light, and no way out, but by showing just a small amount of gratitude it can provide a light at the end of the tunnel.* Acknowledge your feelings, journal about them, sit with your sadness, make friends with your anger, and tell your grief it's ok that it's here. Then alongside that find something to be grateful for while sitting with your emotions and get ready for the next step of changing and correcting your negative thought patterns to positive ones. While it is part of the process of healing to sit with our thoughts and feelings that are negative, we don't want to keep them around for the rest of our life. Just the act of writing or journaling about something that you are grateful for can give your mind and mindset a positive shift to begin this process. It can improve both your cognitive and emotional wellbeing.

Acknowledge/Accept Practice:

A foundational practice for healing grief can include journaling. In journaling you witness your own vulnerable self and become your own healer, counselor, and guide as you acknowledge and accept your true feelings. Often as we deepen into the practice, other feelings such as courage and strength that we need to propel us forward can be uncovered just beneath the negative emotions.

Try these writing prompts and allow yourself to write all of what you are feeling right now until you are done writing, then move on to the next prompt that draws you.

I am angry because...

I am hurt because...

I am sad because...

I am afraid that...

The hardest moments are when...

What I miss the most is...

My favorite memory is...

An unexpected, yet beautiful moment happened when...

The love and good I still have in my life are...

What I know deep down is...

What I am most thankful for today is...

Acknowledge:

I should know enough about loss to realize that you never really stop missing someone--you just learn to live around the huge gaping hole of their absence. ~Alyson Noel

---

I lost my loved one, but what I get to keep with me is...

When having a bad day, how does it feel to acknowledge to yourself: "I'll be Ok, just not today..."

What healing moment do you most need to acknowledge or remember in your journal today?

How do you feel as you read the quote below?

You will lose someone you can't live without, and your heart will be badly broken, and the bad news is that you never completely get over the loss of your beloved. But this is also the good news. They live forever in your broken heart that doesn't seal back up. And you come through. It's like having a broken leg that never heals perfectly-- that still hurts when the weather gets cold, but you learn to dance with the limp.

~Anne Lamott

Accept:

Meditation practice isn't about trying
to throw ourselves away and become
something better. It's about
befriending who we are already.
~Pema Chödrön

What has been the hardest thing to accept about this loss?

What has been a phrase that you absolutely can't stand regarding grief? (It's safe to let your true feelings out here – no judgement, just acceptance of where you are in your process)

What was the most helpful thing someone said to you as you have been grieving?

Why was it so helpful? What feeling did it convey to
you that you needed most at the time?

Chapter 7 -
C- Change and Correct

Between stimulus and response. There is a space. In that space is our power to choose our response. In our response lies our growth and our freedom.

~Viktor Frankl

As we discussed earlier in this book, our mindset is just our beliefs that we think over and over in our minds. They are actually very powerful beliefs. They are thoughts and concepts inside your mind, our set of beliefs, usually developed in childhood and these beliefs determine how we approach and react to the world around us throughout our life. It is what we truly believe. Everything begins with our mindset and branches out from you into your surroundings, family and friends. Our mind is programmed to automatically go to the thoughts and feelings that are most familiar to us. And when we are grieving, the pain is so great that our mind is flooded with such negative thoughts and feelings as worry, shame, doubt, fear, loneliness, and guilt, to name a few. Our feelings or memories surrounding an event that occurred in our life becomes linked in our mind with either a negative or positive emotion. When we experience a sudden trauma or loss in our life, it is easy for our mindset to get stuck in the endless loops of negative thoughts, especially when the event caused us tremendous pain and suffering.

These thoughts, feelings, and emotions become almost habitual and we don't even realize we are in that never-ending loop of negative thinking and negative self-talk. If we do not change our negative thought patterns it can cause us to emotionally shut down which can lead to depression and anxiety. The truth is only you; have the power to go inside, to recognize those negative thoughts and feelings, and have a choice to change them. Which brings us to the next step in the P.E.A.C.E. method of healing and that is "C". The "C" represents the action of changing and course correcting our negative beliefs and thoughts to positive thoughts. It is very difficult to heal from a place of pain and despair, that is why this step in the process is so important.

I know we have touched on the importance of

journaling already in the book, but I will say it again, journaling is a powerful tool for healing because when we write our thoughts and feelings down, it triggers our brain to recall the events associated with those thoughts and feelings. Our memories are linked to either negative or positive emotions surrounding the events in our lives. I have found that if I write or journal about my thoughts and feelings it helps me to look at them from a different perspective, as an observer rather than as a victim. There is something about writing them down and looking at them to trigger our mind to be open to change. It doesn't have to be a novel; it can be a list of bullet points with your feelings and emotions you are experiencing at the time. Either way it allows our mind to process those emotions and by changing and or course correcting the negative emotions and feelings to positive ones, it allows our mind to reach for more and more positive ones instead. Our positive thoughts and emotions lead to positive feelings and gives our heart a chance to feel them and begin to heal, just one thought and feeling at a time.

Journaling enables me to express my emotions through writing and to organize and visualize those negative thoughts, emotions, and feelings that in the past I would have tried to ignore because it was too painful to face them. I think of it as a way to change or course correct my thoughts and feelings to something more positive and uplifting instead of staying in the loop of negativity and sadness. Journaling in a lot of ways, helps me to understand myself better and what I am actually feeling, and I get a chance to witness my feelings through the act of writing. This simple act of writing helps to focus our mind and cut down on the chaos of the negative thoughts that are swirling around in our head.

This one simple exercise of writing down your thoughts, emotions, and feelings can be used as a way of getting into the present moment, gaining control of your thoughts, emotions and feelings, that are constantly replaying over and over again, and reliving the past and change them, through writing them down. I like to make two columns on my paper when I am doing this step of the process, so I can write down my negative thoughts, emotions and feelings in the moment in one column and in the other column I write down positive thoughts, emotions, and feelings to replace them with. I then say them out loud as an affirmation to trigger my mind to accept and change them. In a similar way, journaling would allow you to brainstorm new ways to cope with the loss and set attainable small goals to accomplish throughout the process of transforming your mindset and life.

If you think that finding things to be grateful for is difficult, then start by questioning yourself. Ask yourself, *'what could I be grateful for?'* Search for this answer within yourself rather than asking others. At first, you will be blank as a canvas. But as you ask this question every day, you will eventually start finding answers to this question, and *slowly the blank canvas will fill with different hues of positivity.* As for me, I started changing my negative thoughts to those of being grateful for my children, grandchildren, and family and then I began to find other things to be grateful for like my health and so on.

The best way to practice the P.E.A.C.E. method and gratitude is by setting aside some time at the beginning or end of your day. Invest this time in yourself for healing and to acknowledge and accept your current thoughts and feelings and begin to change those thoughts and feelings to more positive ones by recalling all the good things that happen to you each day. If you are journaling, then write down whatever you are grateful for that day. I highly recommend journaling as a way to remind ourselves what we are grateful for each day. You will be amazed at how much you change your mindset just by replacing those negative thoughts with positive ones.

If the only prayer you ever say in your entire life
is thank you, it will be enough.
~Meister Eckhart

As you are in the process of sitting quietly with your thoughts and feelings you might want to highlight all the moments of your day that made you happy and brought a smile to your face, or simply made you feel thankful to have another day of your life. This will help bring back a sense of contentment and pleasure and will help you change and replace those negative thoughts and feelings with more enjoyable positive ones. If we look hard and deep enough, we can always find something to be grateful for in the midst of our pain. It can be anything. Even if it is just that we have a roof over our head and food to eat that day, it's enough to be grateful for. In order to have long-lasting change that heals us we have to divert our mind from all the negative thoughts and feelings such as shame, worry, doubt, fear, loneliness, and guilt. By changing and replacing these negative thoughts, and feelings with more positive ones, it will lead to a happy and more purposeful life.

The conscious act of journaling and being aware of our thoughts and feelings, whether negative or positive will aid in the healing process and help us pull ourselves out of the looping negative thought patterns that unconsciously plague us. Once we begin to change and course correct our negative thoughts and feelings and replace them with more positive ones we can continue with the last step of the P.E.A.C.E. method, the "E" – Expand and Elevate, which is where we take those new positive thoughts and build on them with more positive ones. What we feed our mind and in this case with positive thoughts and feelings, will expand and our mind will begin to look for more positive thoughts which leads to positive feelings and an elevated, more joyous mood and overall happier life. If this is what you are looking for then keep reading and let's expand and elevate those new positive thoughts and feelings to continue healing our hearts and ultimately change our life to learn to live again.

Change/Correct Practice:

Current negative thoughts and feelings	Replace with positive thoughts and feelings

Change:

*When thinking about life remember
this: no amount of guilt can solve the
past and no amount of anxiety can
change the future. ~Anonymous*

Where have you been carrying the most guilt or anxiety?

What is one small piece of guilt or anxiety that you are ready to change or let go of?

Correct:

Quiet the voice telling you to do more,

and trust that in this moment, who you

are, where you are at and what you

are doing is enough. You will get to

where you need to be in your own

time. Until then, breathe. Breathe and

be patient with yourself and your

process. You are doing the best you

can to cope and survive amid your

struggles, and that's all you can ask of

yourself. It's enough. You are enough.

~Daniell Koepke

Where have your own expectations of yourself been too high?

What would it feel like to tell yourself that your best is good enough? Can you gift that to yourself right now?

Chapter 8 -
E- Elevate and Expand

The secret of change is to focus all of your energy, not on

fighting the old but on building the new.

~Socrates

Throughout this book we have discussed a lot about how our thoughts and beliefs determine our mindset which in turn determines our emotions and feelings, which ultimately determines our mood, personality, our state of being and how we show up in the world. In the last chapter, we began to start to change and course correct our negative thoughts and feelings and emotions by replacing them with more positive thoughts and feelings. Now in this chapter we continue our process by adding the last step, the "E" in the P.E.A.C.E. method of healing and changing our mindset. In this step we build on those positive thoughts and begin to expand our mindset and look for more positive thoughts and feelings by expanding and elevating our awareness to bring in more positivity. As you sit in quiet prayer and meditation going through each step of the P.E.A.C.E. method, and as you pause, examine, accept, and change your negative thoughts and feelings to more positive ones, then expand on those thoughts, keep going and remember those past happy positive experiences and memories. Now, try to start imagining a new life filled with joy and happiness again. I know this is not easy, and it can seem almost impossible right now when you are in the middle of the grieving process. But even though you are experiencing immense grief, the key to long-lasting, true heart and soul healing begins with you starting to imagine and invent in your mind's eye a new future for yourself. It starts with a small glimpse and grows and expands as you bring more positive thoughts and feelings to your mind to change your mindset and eventually your life.

Keeping a check on your emotions and thoughts is the core of moving on.

When you understand the essence of becoming aware of your thoughts and feelings and steer them towards more positivity, and finding things to be grateful for, you will be able to move towards a better and more productive life. The practice of mindfulness is so important in this step, because by analyzing our present thoughts in every situation and understanding how they connect us to our past, we begin to understand why we have those thoughts and feelings without any judgment. And ironically, by accepting our negative feelings versus resisting, ignoring and pushing them down, it actually helps us to heal and change them to more positive ones. Give that time to yourself, even if it is only 5 minutes a day at first and direct your thoughts towards a more constructive, positive approach to life. Remember, heart and soul level healing takes time. Please don't rush it.

As your body engages in physical wound healing, the last stage is where the new skin forms over it. Healing from the emotional trauma of our grief, works in a similar way. Just like the physical wounds of our bodies heal naturally over time, this step for healing ourselves emotionally takes time and we must allow it to occur naturally. But it starts with consciously choosing to change our mindset and then little by little we change our life by expanding our positive thoughts and continuing to feed our mind positive thoughts and reinforcement. **It is more than just having a positive attitude,** and more than trying to will for something that still makes you uncomfortable to take the pain away. Being positive doesn't mean that you're going to avoid what has already happened. It means that you're going to deal with the sh*t in a particular, step by step way, and when you do; that's where you find healing.

I know it can be difficult to think about something positive or have gratitude at a time in our life when we are surrounded by grief and pain. But I promise you if you can just go deep inside you and focus on one positive thing at a time, and build on each positive thought, it will help you move forward and not stay stuck in the vicious cycle of grief and negative thoughts and feelings.

If you are having trouble elevating and expanding your positive thoughts to more positive thoughts during your meditation then, sit still, close your eyes and imagine you are at a place where you can hear the sound of chirping birds, a waterfall or water running in a stream, or perhaps the soft whistle of the breeze blowing by. How soothing does that sound? Nature has a lot of ways to soothe our pain. Obviously, you can't expect trees to answer your questions, but you can find peace in nature, and that's when you will be able to find answers to your queries. Block out some time for yourself and spend some time alone with nature. Just give yourself time to gently heal as each positive thought and feeling replaces the pain of those all too familiar negative thoughts and feelings.

Maybe you would enjoy taking a walk and breathing in the after-scent of rain, watching the leaves dancing with the breeze, or losing yourself in the sound of the ocean, taking a moment to feel the waves crashing around your feet and claiming the sand beneath you, taking it away. Nature can be one of the best antidotes. Sitting outside on the front porch listening to nature is one of my favorite places to sit and go through the 5 step, P.E.A.C.E. method as I continue to be mindful of my thoughts and feelings in my life. Even though, at the time of this writing, it has been almost 19 years since my husband Chris passed away, I can remember several times when I was grieving and feeling sad and angry, or frustrated that I was drawn to go outside in nature. Ever since I was a little girl, I always liked to take nature walks and be outside.

Back then, I didn't realize that my soul knew how to soothe me and make me feel better just by taking a walk and feeling the wind on my face and admiring all that was around me. Picking wildflowers was another favorite activity I would do when I was upset or just needed some "me" time to gather my thoughts, or in this case to look for more positive things to be grateful for to elevate and expand my thoughts and feelings to make me feel better. As, I look back on my childhood, I remember my mom and my grandmother with big smiles on their faces when I would bring them a bouquet of wildflowers, I had picked for them. I have always enjoyed cheering someone up and putting a smile on their face. So, when my mom and grandmother smiled it would make me happy and I would smile too. Studies have shown that there is something about flowers that naturally brightens our mood and decreases anxiety. Some say the aroma that flowers give off has relaxing and soothing powers. I would have to agree, when I pick a flower and smell its sweet fragrance, I automatically get a smile on my face and my mood is elevated and more positive. Even in winter, although they don't have the sweet fragrance and beautiful colors of spring flowers, you can still create some beautiful bouquets of flowers to sit on your table to brighten your home and elevate your mood to a more positive one.

When we incorporate the mindfulness practices of the 5 step, P.E.A.C.E. method into our daily lives, we purposefully sit quietly in prayer and meditation, with the goal to bring ourselves to focus on something without losing it. When we focus our mind entirely on something, our brain stops wandering around- that's mindfulness. Being mindful is one of the best practices we can do to divert and change our negative thoughts and feelings that lead to depression and anxiety and move towards more positive thoughts and feelings which leads to joy and happiness in our life. These five simple, mindful steps of the P.E.A.C.E. method can lead you from a place of darkness and sorrow to a place of peace, where joy and happiness can be found again. I believe using the tips and tools of the P.E.A.C.E. method for mindful healing, and shifting our mindset, is a wonderful way to connect our heart and our mind and leads to long lasting soulful healing. Use and practice the steps of the P.E.A.C.E. method anytime you need to feel better and have a more positive mindset and mood.

Be mindful of your mind to heal your heart!

Elevate/Expand Practice:

Find something to feel good about and
get out of the way and allow the cells
to receive what they've been asking
for. That is the key to healing.
~Esther Hicks

Take a moment right now and reach for the highest thought that makes you feel good.

Allow yourself to bask in this beautiful thought as you would in sunshine for as long as it feels good to do so.

Then move on with your day as usual and note any expanding positive feelings as you practice this every morning before starting your day or before going to sleep at night.

Elevate:

Do you believe the quote above? How does it make you feel?

What would it feel like if you chose to elevate your own thoughts by believing, if only for a moment that it was true?

What is the most empowering thought or idea you can imagine about yourself or your life at this point?

Expand:

As a single footstep will not make a
path on the earth, so a single thought
will not make a pathway in the mind.
To make a deep physical path, we
walk again and again. To make a deep
mental path, we must think over and
over the kind of thoughts we wish to
dominate our lives.
~Henry David Thoreau

What new thoughts have you been thinking lately to help create and expand a new, more positive mental path for yourself?

Chapter 9 -
Obstacles We Face

It's going to get harder before it gets easier. But it will get better. You just have to make it through the hard stuff first.

~Donthula Saicharan

We face many different obstacles throughout our lifetime, and I know you may not want to hear this right now, but the words in the above quote are the truth. The journey of moving forward in our life after we suffer such a great loss as losing our spouse, or an important loved one suddenly can be like climbing a mountain with no clear view of the top. As Donthula states in his quote above *'you have to make it through the hard stuff first.'* And it starts with one step at a time, and even small steps count. Since the loss of your spouse or loved one, I suspect the words you must've heard the most from the people who care about you is *'you need to move on...'* But the real question is, do we ever really move on? Or is it just a figment of our imagination? The point is, moving on isn't an overnight process, nor is it a linear path. There are stages of moving on and grieving, and we must've all heard about them, even subtly. You start your healing journey by making a decision, and taking the first step, then the second, then the third, and you just keep going forward. However, this is not the actual scenario that most of us live as we travel along the twists and turns of our grief journey.

The truth is that obstacles are going to arise when we are changing and growing through our pain, and that's the nature of change. And actually, your healing journey through grief will be much more like a winding road than a straight or linear path. The old saying "change is hard even if it is for the best" holds true here. It was the painful obstacles along my healing journey that guided me to mindfulness and becoming aware of my thoughts and feelings. It was there in my deepest dark moments of my grief journey that I discovered the P.E.A.C.E method as a way to consciously change my thoughts. And you know as I consciously started acknowledging my negative thoughts and feelings and then purposefully changing and course correcting them to more and more positive ones, I began to become more grateful and amazingly my life began to change for the better.

Anytime we embark on a journey to change something about ourselves we will face obstacles that could keep us from achieving what we set out to do. Changing our mindset from negative to positive is no different. If anything, I think it may be harder to change our mindset than most other things we may want to accomplish in our life. Why, do you ask? Well, remember when we discussed earlier that our mindset was made up of our beliefs and our beliefs were an accumulation of our past memories? How old we are when we come to the realization that we need to change our mindset in order to live a happier and more joyous life will drastically impact the intensity of our obstacles. If we are in our 50's, then we have fifty years of old memories and beliefs that could possibly come up for us and sabotage us when we are trying to change our life.

Contrary to common belief, moving on when we are grieving is more like a roller-coaster ride. There are ups and downs, unexpected turns, and dips along the journey. Just when you think you are fine and you are at the peak of positivity, a sudden dip in the path forces you to fall face-first to the bottom. The point is, you will move forward, with all the emotions and all the memories. And despite enduring such a huge loss, you come out as a much stronger person. As we overcome our negative mindset of grief and navigate the obstacles to a more positive life, we find the joy and happiness we once had, but it is different now.

One of the most common obstacles we face as we look grief and fear in the face is that we often suppress our grief. We refrain ourselves from crying, from asking for help, from merely opening up. We think we 'should' be done, or over it or have moved on by now. It does us more harm than good. These emotions are stuck somewhere in our brain or in our body and come back with full force. We may hear a song connected to our memories with that person or get a whiff of their cologne randomly as we pass through the streets. This happens in grief. It can even happen years later and then flood you with tears. It's okay to feel that way. It's okay to reminisce about the memories of our loved ones and let ourselves cry through the pain of that loss. *It's ok to cry sometimes.* But what's not okay is to allow our grief and pain to overcome us and stop living our life. We need to fight those painful feelings and the negative thoughts of our grief mindset and take the necessary steps to change them and heal in order to move forward with our life, the best we can.

As we are navigating our way through this uncharted territory and painful time in our life, most of us don't have any idea of how we are going to react, we have no idea of the obstacles we will face. No matter how tough we are, there are no set rules according to which we react. There are going to be a lot of times when you will be churning with turmoil and begin to feel the magnitude of your loss. This turmoil will trigger you and you will experience such emotions as sadness, anger, guilt and shame– to name a few, and they will vary in intensity and just know that this is normal. Just don't be too hard on yourself. You may feel or experience such physical signs as feeling sick to your stomach, dizzy, numb, tired all the time, and/or an emptiness deep down inside that you can't explain. It's important to understand that it will take time and you will have to get through one obstacle at a time to move forward.

The moment you decide to stand tall in front of your pain, you are ready to enter in this roller-coaster ride. Hold fast, though, because this ride of overcoming grief is everchanging and is not going to end soon. But it will shape you into a much stronger and more compassionate person. You will need to consciously choose to step out of your *'eat-cry-sleep-repeat cycle.'* But, by learning and implementing the five steps in the P.E.A.C.E method, and the accompanying tools, you can overcome those obstacles and create a life you love again, Peace by Piece. By changing your mindset, you change your life.

Chapter 10 - Conclusion

Moving on doesn't mean you forget about things. It just means you have to accept what happened and continue living.

~Erza Scarlet

Throughout the previous chapters of this book, you have learned how to become aware of your thoughts and how to change them to more positive ones by implementing the steps of the P.E.A.C.E. method. My hope is that you will use these simple tips and tools to light your path and grow through your grief and overcome the darkness surrounding you in that place of despair. No one can understand the pain and suffering of grief unless they have experienced the journey. You are braver and stronger than you think you are, and I believe in you. You have come so far, don't stop now, you are on your way to healing your heart and your mind, and by taking one step at a time, you are moving out of your grief and into a beautiful future filled with love and happiness.

As now you are moving forward along your journey, it becomes vitally important to believe in yourself. Believe that you deserve to be happy. Believe that things will get better. Believe that your suffering will end, and you will find your way through this painful time. Value yourself and treat yourself as you would a sick person until you are feeling more well. For a lot of people, this is the hardest part, but this is an essential ingredient to your healing as well. You might be filled with negative thoughts or self-doubt, and that's ok, but you can't expect someone else to treat you better than you treat yourself. It starts with you.

I believe that our culture portrays grief as a terrifying mess of emotions that needs to be cleaned up and tossed off as soon as possible. The idea is that it is something to fix, but it isn't. It is rather something to support and nurture until we can heal through it. Our cultural ideas about grief keep us from caring for ourselves while still living and managing our grief. It keeps us away from being able to support who we love. It's even worse when these outdated ideas add suffering on top of our pain. I saw a quote the other day by an unknown author that I think really sums the grief journey up quite nicely, it said, *"Grief never ends, but it changes. It's not a place to stay. Grief is not a sign of weakness, nor a lack of faith. It is the price of love."* As I reflect back along my journey through grief, I can see how those words ring true. I was so buried in my grief and hurt and anger that I forgot to be grateful for the seemingly short amount of time I had with Chris.

It might hurt in the beginning to become aware of your thoughts and feelings surrounding your grief, but later on, you will start feeling better. You will still miss your loved one; however, the memories will bring a smile to your face. Because our mind is trying to heal, the painful memories often get shifted to the background, and we find ourselves remembering and longing for the good times. But, once we stop and take the time to sit with our thoughts, feelings, and emotions to heal them, we slowly begin to forget what was hurting us and start living with what is actually present. The more you suppress your emotions, the more it will hurt you. Keeping it all inside is like staying inside a mirror maze. You can't look past yourself and the confined surroundings unless you step out of that maze. Similarly, if you keep your emotions bottled up inside yourself, you will never be able to look beyond your pain to see a new future.

Learning to be present in the moment you are living right now, and you naturally wind up in the positive part of your emotional scale. Being present even just for a little while can help you by allowing you to stop worrying about what has already happened. Using the tips and tools of the P.E.A.C.E. method, will give you a roadmap and make it easier for you to take action to change your mindset and ultimately change your life. You can easily make up your mind to go to the gym or participate in activities that you like. It will help you to bring calm and peace in the middle of this stressful journey.

As of now, you have learned to make peace with your past, and all this brings you to your destination, that is, healing. It is time to motivate yourself and focus on yourself. Plan ahead. Visualize yourself achieving the goals that you planned to achieve before you lost your important loved one. Use the same power of emotions that once pulled you down to plan your future and get it going.

Now that you have put up with the rain,

the rainbow awaits to light your way.

As you begin moving forward to the next stage in your life, it is time to pick up your own pieces under the light and look ahead. This is the time when you start recalling every moment with a smile. This is the time to find your strength and start living with mindfulness to create a legacy for you and your family. Again, everything begins and ends with our mindset. What new mindset do you need to adopt today, at this very moment to get you through today? Motivate yourself to get through the bad today by playing a game on your mind that is the game of good. Tell yourself that good is surely going to come tomorrow. If not tomorrow, then very soon. Think positive and observe the changes and progress along your journey. This, too, shall pass. Allow light in the middle of the darkness to illuminate your path through grief.

Afterword

Every step taken in mindfulness brings us one step closer to healing ourselves and the planet.

~Thich Nhat Hanh

My passion is to help others manage their grief and be able to move forward and heal much faster than I did. I am still healing, but I have a healthier mindset now. I have healed through a lot of the pain and suffering I had been holding on to in the past and the life I lost for many years. I am happy now and learning to love my life again. You may need a gentle nudge to push yourself forward. I pray that the steps of the P.E.A.C.E. method will give you that nudge and help you to gain extra miles on your healing journey. Your goal, going forward, should be looking towards a better tomorrow. Every sunrise holds the possibility of a fresh start, and you get to choose. Remember, everything begins with your mindset and branches out from you. Only you have the power to go inside it and change it. Should you need deeper, one on one support or guidance through your grief process, I offer several programs that can help you.

Email: dr-roneisa@thecourageprocess.com

"The lotus is the most beautiful flower. whose petals
open one by one. But it will only grow in the mud.
In order to grow and gain wisdom. first. we must
have the mud - the obstacles
in life and suffering.....
The mud speaks of the common ground
that humans share.
no matter what our situations in life.....
Whether we have it all or we have nothing.
we are all faced with the same
obstacles: sadness. loss. illness.
dying. and death.
If we are to strive as human beings to gain more
wisdom. more kindness. and more compassion. we must
have the intention to grow as a lotus and
open each petal one by one."
~Goldie Hawn

About the Author

Dr. Roneisa Matero is a veteran, nationally certified family nurse practitioner, grief expert, certified health and wellness coach as well as a certified life coach, with over 30 years of experience in helping and serving others. Roneisa joined the USAF in August 1990 just after graduating from high school. She spent 5 years as an EMT- flight medic serving her country. During that time, she was deployed to England, Italy, Turkey, and Saudi Arabia during the Gulf War before she took an early discharge in May 1995 to take care of her family and further her education as a registered nurse. Roneisa received her Bachelorette degree as a registered nurse in 1997 from the University of Arkansas for Medical Sciences before having her second child a month later and moving to North Carolina.

She returned to college in September 1998 to pursue her master's degree in Nursing as a Family Nurse Practitioner at Duke University and graduated with honors in May of 2000. It wasn't until May 2014 she again returned to college to pursue her doctoral degree in nursing and graduated with honors from Maryville University, earning her Doctor of Nursing Practice degree in May 2016.

Roneisa has been widowed since August 7, 2002 and has immersed herself in raising her children and dealing with the loss of her husband and father to her children. She lost her husband, a Combat Controller in the Air Force, tragically in a plane crash along with 9 other United States Air Force service members.

Roneisa has been in the medical field and helping people for the past 30 years. First as a flight medic in the USAF, then as a registered nurse and a family nurse practitioner. Her career gave her the means to go on and support and raise her children. During her journey through grief, she realized she wanted to help others who are searching for ways to heal and move forward while managing the crippling effects of grief.

Roneisa has helped hundreds of people throughout the years to deal with various aspects of the grief process and the trials and tribulations associated with grieving the loss of a spouse or loved one. She has lived and experienced the grief and pain that comes with losing a spouse and being left alone to raise children. After her youngest child, Dante got married and left home in 2016, she decided to give in to her long-time desire to write a book that would help widows with children cope with the grief and loss. She was inspired to write a book that she wished she had had all those years ago when her life suddenly was turned upside down and she was left to raise her two small children alone. Her first book titled "It Takes Courage: The young widow's guide to grieving and raising children alone" was published in 2020.

Roneisa is passionate about helping others who are trying to pick up the pieces, heal their broken hearts and put their life back together after losing a loved one. She is a grief expert and teaches her clients genuine, simple techniques to start healing from their grief and learn to live again in a healthier more positive way.

Roneisa lives in a small town in east Texas close to her two children and two wonderful grandchildren. She currently teaches and mentors doctoral students as an adjunct professor for Abilene Christian University, and Walden University in the Doctor of Nursing practice programs, and she works part-time as a family nurse practitioner. She enjoys taking long walks along a beautiful beach or in the mountains to connect with nature, writing, but most of all she loves spending quality time with her family and helping others any way she can.

To connect with Roneisa:
Facebook: The Empowered Widow
Website: https://thecourageprocess.com/
Email: dr-roneisa@thecourageprocess.com

Other books by Dr. Roneisa:

It Takes Courage: The Young Widow's Guide to Grieving and Raising Children Alone

Peace by Piece: A Companion Journal for the Grieving Process

About the Publisher

Positive Energy Publications
making the world a little brighter...one book at a time

More titles by Positive Energy Publications:

How to Organize with Ease: Easy to Follow Steps for Garages, Closets, Junk Drawers and More...

7 Simple Steps to Non-Toxic Gardening: A Guide for the Overwhelmed, Eco-Conscious, First-Time Gardener

Rivers of Change Channels of Hope: A Mental Health Survivor's Guide Through Lived Experience

Finding your Soulmate after 40: The Smart Woman's Guide

Navigating Career Changes after 40: The Soulful Woman's Guide

30 Days to Happier Ways: The Journal

30 Days to Simpler Ways: The Journal

Positive Energy Oracle Cards: Companion Guide

Unleash your Intuitive Superpowers

#BrokenHearted Wisdom

#WholeHearted Wisdom

#WholeHearted Wisdom – Poetic Journal

3,2,1 No More Pain

Pause, Reset, and Recharge: A Self-Compassion Guide for Mindful Recovery

PositiveEnergyPublications.com